W9-CRS-296

FIVE-MINUTE WARMUPS

FOR THE PRIMARY GRADES

Quick-and-Easy Activities To Reinforce
Basic Skills

by Bea Green, Sandi Schlichting, and Mary Ellen Thomas

Incentive Publications, Inc.
Nashville, Tennessee

Illustrated by Doris Wasserman
Cover by Doris Wasserman
Edited by Jan Keeling

ISBN 0-86530-264-2

Copyright © 1994 by Incentive Publications, Inc., Nashville, TN. All rights reserved. No part of this publication may be reproduced, stored in a retrieval system, or transmitted in any form or by any means (electronic, mechanical, photocopying, recording, or otherwise) without written permission from Incentive Publications, Inc., with the exception below.

Pages labeled with the statement © 1994 by Incentive Publications, Inc., Nashville, TN are intended for reproduction. Permission is hereby granted to the purchaser of one copy of FIVE-MINUTE WARMUPS FOR THE PRIMARY GRADES to reproduce these pages in sufficient quantities for meeting the purchaser's own classroom needs.

PRINTED IN THE UNITED STATES OF AMERICA

Table of Contents

LANGUAGE

BONUS: SELF-AWARENESS ACTIVITIES

PREFACE

How many times have you realized that you have just five or ten minutes left before it's time to take your students to lunch, to the media center, or outside for P.E.? Or perhaps you've just finished a terrific reading lesson, and find that there are five minutes to go before your teammate is ready to change classes!

It may not be possible to eliminate those extra five-minute periods even with the best of planning, but five minutes a day adds up to over fifteen hours of instructional time in a school year. We believe those odd extra moments can be put to excellent use with little or no preparation at all! *Five-Minute Warmups for the Primary Grades* provides the key to using lag times for effective reinforcement of math, social studies, and language skills and concepts.

These activities are more than just ways to fill in odd moments. Many of the activities help students "stretch" basic skills and knowledge. Some can be used as great lead-ins for new units. Others are meant for drill or for review of basic skills and facts. You will find that many of the activities can be extended into full-length lessons.

At the back of the book is a bonus section of self-awareness activities. These can be used at the beginning of school to help students become acquainted, or any time as instant activities that help improve self-esteem. They even work well for those times when the students need a little relaxation and fun while learning, too!

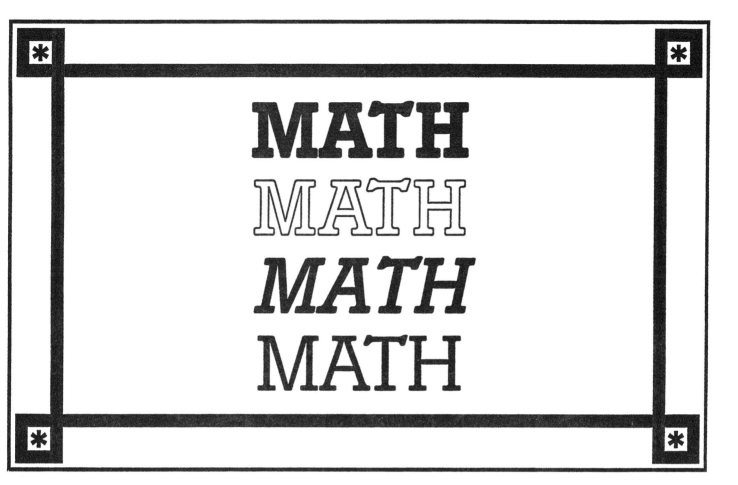

MATH
MATH
MATH
MATH

NUMBER ACTIONS

Let students practice silent counting in a fun way. Select a number between one and seventy-five. Write it on the board or just announce it aloud. Then choose one of the actions below to be performed by the students that many times. Students can be selected individually to perform the action while silently counting the number of times, or the whole class can participate at once. If the action is done by individual students, the rest of the class can determine if the action was done the correct number of times.

Actions to try:
* jumping jacks
* hopping on one leg
* knee bends
* shaking hands with someone nearby
* turning completely around
* hand-clapping
* touching toes
* nodding heads

© 1994 by Incentive Publications, Inc., Nashville, TN.

COUNT OR MEASURE?

Ask students whether they would count or measure a variety of objects you name. If their answer is "measure," ask them to name the device they would use to do the measuring.

Here is a list of items to start with:

* eggs (count)
* bag of sugar (measure . . . with cup or with scale)
* temperature of water (measure . . . with thermometer)
* length of sidewalk (measure . . . with ruler or meter-stick)
* days in a month (count)
* shoes in the classroom (count)

© 1994 by Incentive Publications, Inc., Nashville, TN.

WORKING MATH

Students need to be aware that they are learning math facts and skills that they can use in real life, not just in math class. Ask them to decide how math skills (and even which math skills) would be put to work in the following situations:

* You have to share a bag of candy with three friends.
* Mom sends you to the store to buy a loaf of bread.
* You wonder if you have enough money to buy a new toy you see.
* You don't want to miss a special program on TV tonight.
* You are trying to buy a can of soda from a vending machine.
* You want to turn in to the bank your bagful of pennies for dimes.

© 1994 by Incentive Publications, Inc., Nashville, TN.

SYMBOL TRUTH

Write one of these symbols on the chalkboard:

> < =

Have students come to the board and place numbers on either side of the symbol to make a true math statement. Demonstrate with one or two examples to illustrate the idea:

$5 = 3 + 2$ $5 < 6$ $6 > 3$

© 1994 by Incentive Publications, Inc., Nashville, TN.

WHAT'S WRONG?

Write a problem and answer on the board. Make sure that the answer is incorrect. Let students tell what is wrong with the problem. Write answers that would indicate forgetting to borrow, adding instead of subtracting, and so forth.

Another version of this activity would be to put five problems and answers on the board at once. Let students determine which problems have correct answers and which have incorrect answers.

© 1994 by Incentive Publications, Inc., Nashville, TN.

SIZE WISE

Let students practice ordering objects by size with this activity.

Ask them to line up on one side of the room by height, tallest to shortest or shortest to tallest. Or, ask the girls to line up by height on one side of the room. Ask the boys to line up by height on the other side of the room. Then let them merge the two lines into one.

Have students stack their textbooks on top of their desks or tables. The largest book should be on the bottom of the stack and the smallest book should be on top of the stack.

Can they stack their books according to how thick they are?

© 1994 by Incentive Publications, Inc., Nashville, TN.

OPERATIONS

List on the board several problems like the ones below. Leave off all signs to identify the operations that complete the problem with the answer given.

Let students go to the board and write signs that correctly complete each problem.

Examples: 10 ___ 5 = 15   2 ___ 1 = 1   14 ___ 3 = 11

$$
\begin{array}{ccc}
15 & 27 & 11 \\
\underline{7} & \underline{10} & \underline{11} \\
22 & 17 & 22
\end{array}
$$

© 1994 by Incentive Publications, Inc., Nashville, TN.

CALLING TIME

If you have a clock face with movable hands, keep it nearby and do this activity at least twice a week for a few minutes:

Hold the clock in front of the class. Set the hands to 12:00. Let the class call out the time in unison. Move the clock hands ahead in increments of 10 or 15 minutes or by half-hours. Students should call out the time each time it is reset. As the students' skill increases, begin to set the minute hand in between the five-minute increments. You may want to let students reset the clock for the rest of the class.

© 1994 by Incentive Publications, Inc., Nashville, TN.

BONKERS, JR.

This is an easier version of an intermediate game. Go around the room, letting each student say one number (starting with one). The next student says the number two, and so forth. One rule should be stated first: "If it is your turn, and the next number contains a four (or any other specified digit), you must say 'bonkers' instead of the number." Then play continues with the next student.

Example: "Don't say any number with a three in it."
                First child: "One."
                Second child: "Two."
                Third child: "Bonkers."
                Fourth child: "Four."
(13, 23, and 30 would be "Bonkers" also.)

© 1994 by Incentive Publications, Inc., Nashville, TN.

MATH LINE-UP

When it's time to line up your students to go somewhere, do it in one of these ways:

You may get in line when you can name:

* a multiple of five (or any other number you select)
* a factor of a given number
* a math-related word
* a problem with an answer of ____
* a fraction
* a number greater than ____ (or a number less than ____)

© 1994 by Incentive Publications, Inc., Nashville, TN.

MATH LINE-UP II

When it's necessary to have your students line up, let them earn their places in line by naming a number . . .
* . . . with the digit three in it
* . . . that you say when you count by twos
* . . . with digits whose sum is ten

Or by naming something that . . .
* . . . you could measure with a ruler
* . . . is rectangular in shape
* . . . comes in dozens
* . . . has numbers on it (like money)

© 1994 by Incentive Publications, Inc., Nashville, TN.

TURTLE RACE

Quickly divide the class into four teams. Appoint a "turtle" for each team. Line up all the turtles facing a chosen finish line.

Make up a math story problem about turtles and say it aloud. The first team to give the correct answer can have its turtle advance two steps toward the finish line. The team whose turtle reaches the finish line first, or gets closest to the finish line in the playing time, wins.

Sample problems: Three turtles joined a pond of ten turtles. How many turtles are in the pond now?

Twelve turtles started on a walk together, and six turtles decided to go back to the pond. How many turtles stayed on the walk?

© 1994 by Incentive Publications, Inc., Nashville, TN.

TWELVE QUESTIONS

Select a number from one to 100. Write it on a slip of paper to hold in your hand. Let students ask questions about your number. Your answers must be "yes" or "no." Students should try to guess your mystery number in twelve guesses or less.

Good question strategies might include:
* Is it between fifty and 100?
* Is it even or odd?
* Is it a two-digit number?
* Do I say it when I count by fives?

© 1994 by Incentive Publications, Inc., Nashville, TN.

ADD OR SUBTRACT?

This activity allows students to decide whether addition or subtraction was used to arrive at an answer.

Give a starting number. Then give the answer. Students should be able to tell you if you added or subtracted to reach the answer. If you want to have them tell how much was added or subtracted from the original number, that would be even more challenging.

Examples:
* I start with 10. I have 15 for an answer. What did I do? (Add five)
* I start with 12. I have 9 as my answer. What did I do? (Subtract three)

© 1994 by Incentive Publications, Inc., Nashville, TN.

RULER RACE

When your students are restless and need to move around, try this measurement activity.

Give students rulers and challenge them to find things in the room that are:
* almost exactly one foot high, wide, or thick
* less than six inches high, wide, or thick
* more than nine inches, but less than twelve inches, wide

Call "time" after two or three minutes of any one challenge and let students share their findings.

© 1994 by Incentive Publications, Inc., Nashville, TN.

18

SHAPE UP

Give groups of four to six students a long piece of string or yarn (yarn is best). Let the groups spread out around the room. As you call out a shape, the students in each group form that shape with their piece of yarn. Each student in the group should have his or her hands on the yarn, helping to create the desired shape.

Students can form the shapes with the yarn on the floor or in the air.

Try these:

circle	square	triangle	rectangle	oval

How about numbers?

5	2	7	8

© 1994 by Incentive Publications, Inc., Nashville, TN.

PLACE IT

This activity gives students some practice in working with place value in three-digit numbers.

Have students draw three blanks in a row on their papers: ___   ___   ___.

As you call out three digits, each student writes each digit wherever he or she wants to on the blanks. Then ask students to share the numbers they made. What was the biggest number possible? What was the smallest number possible? Share the results.

© 1994 by Incentive Publications, Inc., Nashville, TN.

A DIFFERENT VIEW

"What else can a number be besides a number?"

Ask your students! Write a digit on the board. Give your class three minutes to name all the things it might be if it were not a number. Encourage creativity and "off the wall" answers.

Example: 3
* a crooked road
* half of an eight
* two toes
* a sideways 'W'

© 1994 by Incentive Publications, Inc., Nashville, TN.

DOUBLE DIGITS

Write a two-digit number on the board.

Have the students:
* tell the sum of the two digits
* tell the difference between the two digits
* tell the product of the two digits (if they are learning multiplication facts)

Ask the students to write two-digit numbers where:
* the sum of the digits is eight (or any other sum up to 18)
* the difference between the two digits is ___ (any number from 0 to 9)

© 1994 by Incentive Publications, Inc., Nashville, TN.

RACE TO 25

Students form two teams. The first member of Team A goes to the board and makes the choice to write either "1" or "1" and "2" vertically on the board. The first member of Team B comes to the board and writes either the next consecutive number or the next two consecutive numbers under those already written. The teams continue to send members to the board, adding one or two more consecutive numbers each time. The team whose member writes the number 25 on the board is declared the winner. Play this game several times and watch students begin to develop strategies for winning!

© 1994 by Incentive Publications, Inc., Nashville, TN.

ORDERED NUMBERS

After students have learned to write the numbers from one to 100, let them try this activity:

Each student should write a number on a sheet of paper according to the condition set by you. You might ask them to write numbers between twenty and 100. They should write large enough so that everyone can read their numbers when they hold them up.

After everyone has written the numbers, call all or part of the class to the front of the room. Ask them to line up with their numbers in order. If two students have the same number, they should stand next to each other, not in front or back of each other. Let them sit down and call up another part of the class to order their numbers.

© 1994 by Incentive Publications, Inc., Nashville, TN.

ON TARGET

Have a student name a target number from ten to twenty-five. Other students in the room name numbers of objects that they see. Add the numbers on the board until the target number has been reached. The student that names the last number of items selects the new target number.

Example:
1. Leslie names the number 18.
2. Sue says she sees five blue chairs. Write 5 on the board.
3. Larry says he sees six boys with sneakers on. Add 6 to 5. 11 is the result.
4. Marty says he sees seven girls with hair ribbons. Add 7 to 11.
5. The target number, 18, has been reached.
6. Marty selects a new target number.

© 1994 by Incentive Publications, Inc., Nashville, TN.

CENTS SENSE

Let students use scrap paper if necessary for this activity. Many students will be able to do the computation mentally.

Ask: "How many cents do I have if I have . . ."

* two dimes   * three nickels and one penny
* one quarter   * four dimes and one nickel
* six nickels   * one quarter and one nickel
* twelve pennies   * five nickels and two pennies
* two quarters   * four quarters and one dime

© 1994 by Incentive Publications, Inc., Nashville, TN.

25

TIME FLIES

Young children have difficulty accurately judging the passage of measured time. This activity lets them practice until they have a feel for given periods of time.

Have all students put their heads down on their desks with their eyes closed. Tell them you will say, "Start." Then they are to raise their heads when they think the specified amount of time has passed. Start with fifteen seconds or thirty seconds and work up to three minutes at a time.

© 1994 by Incentive Publications, Inc., Nashville, TN.

UNITS, PLEASE

Make students more aware of standard units of measure by playing these games:
  * Name an item and have the students name the standard unit of measure that would be used for that item.
    Examples:
        flour (pound)
        fabric or ribbon (yards)
        gasoline (gallons or liters)
        canned goods (ounces or grams)

  * Form two teams. One team names an item and the other team has to name the appropriate unit of measure. Go back and forth between the teams. Points could be awarded if you want to extend the game.

© 1994 by Incentive Publications, Inc., Nashville, TN.

GREATER THAN, LESS THAN

Go around the room quickly, calling on one student at a time. Give each a phrase that describes the number you want him or her to name. The student should respond quickly with a number that meets the condition set forth in the phrase. Examples:

Greater than 25   **Greater than 12 + 2**

Less than 99   **Less than 20 - 5**

If you want to increase the difficulty, give two conditions in each phrase: less than twenty-five and more than three.

© 1994 by Incentive Publications, Inc., Nashville, TN.

JUST THE FACTS

Write three to five digits on the board. Choose digits that can be used together to form math facts in addition and subtraction.

Have students call out as many addition or subtraction facts as they can using the digits on the board.

Example:

2, 7, 5	2 + 5 = 7	5 + 2 = 7	7 − 5 = 2	7 − 2 = 5
2, 3, 4, 5, 6	2 + 3 = 5	3 + 2 = 5	2 + 4 = 6	4 + 2 = 6
	6 − 4 = 2	6 − 2 = 4	5 − 3 = 2	5 − 2 = 3

© 1994 by Incentive Publications, Inc., Nashville, TN.

PACKAGE DEALS

As consumers, your students have to learn to discriminate between real bargain prices and phony bargain prices. Sometimes it is just a matter of knowing which size package to select. The king-size package is not always a king-size bargain.

Ask students which of the following package deals are the better bargains:

* ✳ bubblegum: 3 for 10 cents or a king-size bag of 5 for 25 cents

* ✳ ice-cream bars: 25 cents each or a king-size bag of 3 for 1 dollar

* ✳ marbles: small bag of 6 for 15 cents or a king-size bag of 12 for 25 cents

© 1994 by Incentive Publications, Inc., Nashville, TN.

GOOD FIT

Being aware of size and comparing items by size are important math skills for primary students.

* Hold up a shoebox, a cereal box, or other container and ask students to name items that could fit inside it.

* On another day hold up a very small container (a matchbox, a spice bottle, or a small plastic bag). Ask students to name items that could fit in it.

* Ask students to name things that would not fit inside your classroom.

© 1994 by Incentive Publications, Inc., Nashville, TN.

MEASURE IT

Have students measure various things or distances in your room. Instead of using a ruler, have students use a classroom object with which they are familiar as a standard unit.

Some objects to use:
* ✱ a new piece of chalk   ✱ the chalkboard eraser   ✱ crayon box

Some distances to measure:
* ✱ the width of a desk   ✱ the height of the chair seat   ✱ the distance between desks, windows, etc.

© 1994 by Incentive Publications, Inc., Nashville, TN.

IT'S YOUR PROBLEM

Put one of these story problem answers on the board. Call on three different students to invent a story problem to go with it.

Story Problem Answers:

Six red hens	Nine cars remained.
Thirteen eggs left over	Then there were seven cats.
Two cents more	John needed five cents more.
Fourteen dogs in all	Only eleven birds were left.

© 1994 by Incentive Publications, Inc., Nashville, TN.

MOVING ON

Here's a game to practice addition, subtraction, or multiplication problems. Select one student to start the game. That student stands next to the student in the first seat in the room. You call out or show a math problem to both students. The first student to call out the correct answer gets to "Move On" to the next student's desk. (If the standing student wins, he or she moves on. If the seated student wins, he or she exchanges places with the standing student.)

Any student who can make it back to his original starting point can be declared a winner!

© 1994 by Incentive Publications, Inc., Nashville, TN.

IN BETWEEN

Write two numbers on the board. Use numbers that have a difference of at least twenty. Mentally select a number that falls in between the two written numbers. Give your students at least one clue about your mystery number.

Example:
* It has two digits that are the same.
* It is an odd number.
* You say it when you count by twos.

Let students try to guess your number. Keep track of how many guesses it takes to find the mystery number. Can they improve their guessing strategies on the next game?

© 1994 by Incentive Publications, Inc., Nashville, TN.

SKIPPING NUMBERS

Most primary students learn to count by twos pretty easily. Let students play this skipping-numbers game to practice concentration and mental math:

Go around the room. The first student says "one." The next student skips "two" and says "three." The next student skips "four" and says "five." Continue around the room.

Increase the difficulty after using this activity a few times. Let students skip two or three numbers each turn.

© 1994 by Incentive Publications, Inc., Nashville, TN.

SOCIAL STUDIES
SOCIAL STUDIES
SOCIAL STUDIES
SOCIAL STUDIES

MONEY NAMES

Each country has its own currency. See how many of these currencies your students can match with the correct countries. Repeat this activity every couple of weeks and watch their knowledge grow.

Lira ....Italy, San Marino, Vatican City

Yen............Japan

Franc.........Belgium, France

Pound ....Egypt, Great Britain, Ireland

Drachma....Greece

Mark..........Germany

Peso ....Argentina, Bolivia, Cuba, Mexico

Schilling ....Austria, Somalia

Dollar ....Australia, Canada, Jamaica, USA

If students are curious about other countries, send them to the library to do some research and let them share their results.

© 1994 by Incentive Publications, Inc., Nashville, TN.

PICTURE WORDS

Let your students pretend they are making a map of the playground. Give them the following words and let them volunteer to come to the board and draw a symbol of that object, as if it were going to be used on the map legend.

If you have a longer period of time, let each student make a complete set of symbols for a legend on his or her own paper.

Tree	**Baseball Diamond**	**Drinking Fountain**
School Building	**Restroom**	**Hot Dog Stand**
Slide	**Swing Set**	**Sandbox**
Gate	**Fence**	**Bike Rack**

© 1994 by Incentive Publications, Inc., Nashville, TN.

INTERVIEW TIME

Let one student name a famous person from the past. Have other students decide what questions they would ask that person if they were doing a newspaper interview with him or her. Make sure that everyone knows why that person is considered famous before you start discussing the interview.

Some Suggested Persons:

Martha Washington	Amelia Earhart
Betsy Ross	Martin Luther King, Jr.
Paul Revere	John Kennedy
Benjamin Franklin	Susan B. Anthony

© 1994 by Incentive Publications, Inc., Nashville, TN.

GLOBAL AWARENESS

To help students become more familiar with world geography and to give them the opportunity to use globes, try these questions. Allow groups of students to look at globes for three to five minutes while you ask:

✢ How many countries are in Central America?
✢ Of which continent is Egypt a part?
✢ Does the equator pass through South America?
✢ Is Australia north of any land mass?
✢ Name some of the largest countries in the world.

Allow each student to ask a question of the rest of the class.

© 1994 by Incentive Publications, Inc., Nashville, TN.

PRESIDENT'S MONEY

How many of your students can tell you which president's portrait is on each denomination of currency? Let them try to name them all:

$1 ....Washington
$5 ....Lincoln
$10 ....Hamilton
$20 ....Jackson
$50 ....Grant
$100 ......Franklin

Once students have learned these, ask questions like:

✢ How much do I have if I have one Washington and two Lincolns?

✢ How much do I have if I have one Franklin, two Grants, and a Jackson?

© 1994 by Incentive Publications, Inc., Nashville, TN.

NOT MY JOB!

Everyone has certain jobs to do. When someone doesn't do his or her job, it creates problems and more work for someone else.

Have students name jobs that are part of family life. List them on the board as they are named. Then discuss what happens when the family member responsible for each job doesn't do his or her part. Who suffers? How is the entire family affected? What should be done about those who don't do their jobs correctly and on time?

Relate the above discussion to career-related responsibilities. How is it the same on the job? How is it different?

© 1994 by Incentive Publications, Inc., Nashville, TN.

EVEN EXCHANGE

Name an amount of money and tell which bills or coins can be used to make up that amount. Students should name one or more ways to make that same amount using different combinations of bills or coins.

Examples:
+ 25 cents (one quarter . . . two dimes and one nickel . . . five nickels)
+ $3.10 (three one-dollar bills and one dime . . . twelve quarters and two nickels)
+ $10 (one ten-dollar bill . . . one five-dollar bill and five one-dollar bills)

This practice can be extended at an independent center if you have a supply of play bills and coins. Just write different amounts on index cards and let students see how many different ways they can make each amount.

© 1994 by Incentive Publications, Inc., Nashville, TN.

DOLLAR SENSE

Kids are often unaware of the actual cost of items that they use all the time. Since they are not usually responsible for the purchase of the items, they seldom see the prices.

Name a few items that kids use frequently and let them see how close they can come to naming the correct price. Be sure to use items that you know the price of, or have students find out the prices and report back to the class.

You might use:

- ✤ current fad toys (popular dolls, video games, etc.)
- ✤ cost of a movie ticket
- ✤ cost of a pound of meat
- ✤ cost of popular brand of athletic shoes
- ✤ amount of money spent on classroom supplies per child

© 1994 by Incentive Publications, Inc., Nashville, TN.

AT YOUR SERVICE

Even students can provide services. If you were to set up a student service bureau at your school, what could your students do? Ask your class to list as many services as they can. Here's a list to get you started:

- empty trash cans
- file papers
- clean desks, chalkboards
- tutor younger students
- care for classroom pets

- shelve library books
- show visitors around
- deliver messages
- put up bulletin boards
- make morning announcements

© 1994 by Incentive Publications, Inc., Nashville, TN.

NEEDS OR WANTS?

Help students distinguish between needs and wants. Name the items below, one at a time. Let students respond with "need" or "want":

- shoes
- computer
- television

- prescription drug
- candy bar
- video games

- home/shelter
- textbooks
- newspaper

Be sure to allow discussion of any item upon which students do not agree. Make a "needs" and "wants" bulletin board. Encourage students to add items to it.

© 1994 by Incentive Publications, Inc., Nashville, TN.

WHOSE PROPERTY?

Review the definitions of public and private property.

Private Property: property owned by individuals or groups of individuals
Public Property: property owned by all the people for everyone's use

Read the items on the following list and let your students respond with "public" or "private":

Yellowstone National Park   Statue of Liberty

Little League Ball Park   Community Swimming Pool

Sears Stores   Jones Brothers' BMX Bike Track

School Playground   K-Mart Stores

© 1994 by Incentive Publications, Inc., Nashville, TN.

IN THE KNOW

Being a wise consumer means being a responsible consumer. One important responsibility of a good consumer is knowing what questions to ask about products that are being considered for purchase.

Have students decide what to ask and what to look for as they consider purchasing these items:

New bicycle: Does it come assembled? What kind of guarantee is there? Where do I buy parts for it? Is it the right size for me?

Home computer: Are there instruction manuals with it? Does everything I need come with it? Will it do more than play games? How can I get service for it? Is the price competitive with similar computers?

A pair of jeans: How well are they made? Do they require special cleaning care? Do they fit really well? Will they shrink? Are they too "faddish"? Are they worth the price being asked?

© 1994 by Incentive Publications, Inc., Nashville, TN.

ECONOMICS A–Z

Choose one of the following ideas, and let students name items for every letter of the alphabet.

- ✢ products that you could survive without
- ✢ products that are advertised on television
- ✢ items worth about one dollar
- ✢ products you could not survive without
- ✢ services offered in your community
- ✢ products that probably won't be around in ten years

© 1994 by Incentive Publications, Inc., Nashville, TN.

SPOTLIGHT ON YOU

Role playing is an easy way for students to formulate ideas. Tell them to put themselves in these situations. Call on various students to do the role playing.

- ✢ You are a forest ranger. What should you tell people about the importance of preserving our forests?

- ✢ You are a foreign child visiting the United States. What do you want to find out about this land?

- ✢ You are living in the year 2000. Tell about the sources of energy that you use.

- ✢ You are living on a small island. A ship with 5000 people lands on your island and all 5000 decide to stay. How do you feel?

© 1994 by Incentive Publications, Inc., Nashville, TN.

YOUR CHOICE

People have to make choices about how to spend their time and how to spend their money. When you give up something for something else, the thing you give up is called the "opportunity cost" of the item you chose.

Let students practice making choices and recognizing the opportunity costs of those choices by responding to these questions:

♣ You have $25. You need a new shirt for the PTA play, and you need a new tire for your bike. Which do you choose? What is the opportunity cost?

♣ You are invited to a friend's birthday party on the same day that your brother is playing in the championship ball game. Where will you go? What will be your opportunity cost?

© 1994 by Incentive Publications, Inc., Nashville, TN.

GOODS OR SERVICES?

Discuss briefly the definitions of goods and services.

Goods: things you can touch which are made by humans.

Services: work done by people which usually does not produce things we can touch (teaching, mowing grass)

Let each student who wants to participate tell what his or her parents (or guardians) do for a living. The rest of the class should decide whether the parents (guardians) provide goods or services. If there is disagreement, refer to the definitions above.

© 1994 by Incentive Publications, Inc., Nashville, TN.

BRANDED

Advertisers want you to remember their products. How effective are they? See how many brands students can recall for the following items:

ketchup	fast food places
paper towels	airlines
soft drinks	service stations
breakfast cereals	department stores
types of gum	snack foods
pain relievers	grocery stores

© 1994 by Incentive Publications, Inc., Nashville, TN.

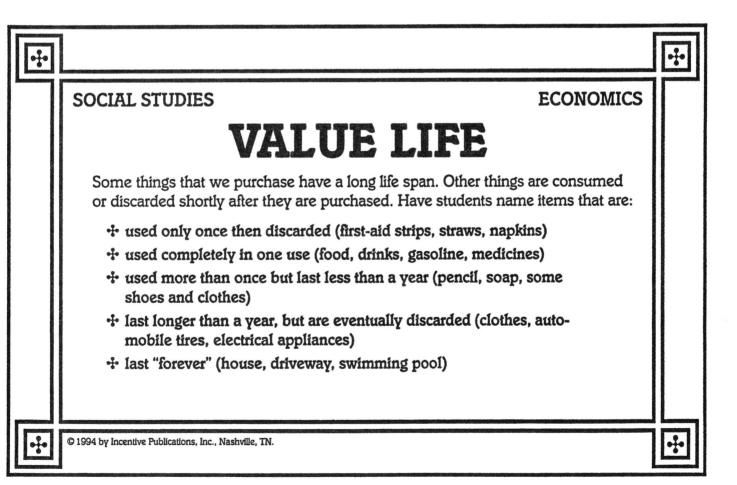

VALUE LIFE

Some things that we purchase have a long life span. Other things are consumed or discarded shortly after they are purchased. Have students name items that are:

+ used only once then discarded (first-aid strips, straws, napkins)

+ used completely in one use (food, drinks, gasoline, medicines)

+ used more than once but last less than a year (pencil, soap, some shoes and clothes)

+ last longer than a year, but are eventually discarded (clothes, automobile tires, electrical appliances)

+ last "forever" (house, driveway, swimming pool)

© 1994 by Incentive Publications, Inc., Nashville, TN.

THUMBS UP, THUMBS DOWN

Read these statements to your students. Have them show "thumbs up" if they agree with the statement and "thumbs down" if they disagree with the statement.

✛ Everyone should dress alike.

✛ Corn is the best vegetable.

✛ You should be allowed to choose your own bedtime.

✛ Teachers don't understand kids.

✛ It is unfair for some people to have more money than others.

✛ Parents who spank their children are cruel.

✛ Everyone should learn to like broccoli.

✛ School should be year-round, not just ten months a year.

© 1994 by Incentive Publications, Inc., Nashville, TN.

NO MONEY

Review the definition of barter with your class:

> *Barter* is the direct exchange of goods or services for other goods or services without the use of money.

Let students tell what goods or services they could exchange for any of the following goods or services provided by their parents:

a trip to the beach	a new baseball glove
a party for their friends	a trip to Disneyland
a special outfit for a party	a pet
a new compact disc	help with homework
transportation to a friend's house	

© 1994 by Incentive Publications, Inc., Nashville, TN.

IT ALL DEPENDS

Discuss the interdependence of jobs and products. Then name one of the following situations and have students name all the jobs and products that would be affected by the situation.

- ✤ No one wants to drink milk anymore.
- ✤ All of the world's tomato crops fail.
- ✤ All fresh water becomes contaminated with salt water.
- ✤ Rock music is banned from all public places.
- ✤ A uniform of black pants and white shirts is required to be worn by everyone at school and at work.
- ✤ Schools will be open only one or two days a week.

© 1994 by Incentive Publications, Inc., Nashville, TN.

48

TRACE IT

To help students realize that goods do not usually come straight from resources to consumers, let them trace one of the following products from raw materials to finished product. Keep them on track if they tend to skip steps in the process.

an ice-cream bar	automobile
front door of house	shirt
jug of milk	computer
notebook paper	football
textbook	radio

© 1994 by Incentive Publications, Inc., Nashville, TN.

ON LINE

Many products are produced on assembly lines where each worker has one specialized job to do toward completion of the product.

Have students decide what workers would be needed to produce these products on an assembly line:

homemade lemonade   laminated placemats

Halloween masks   chocolate chip cookies

autograph books   peanut butter sandwiches

banana splits   terrariums with plants and insects

© 1994 by Incentive Publications, Inc., Nashville, TN.

LANGUAGE

LANGUAGE

LANGUAGE

LANGUAGE

THE INSIDE STORY

Quickly review the parts of a textbook:

title page	body of book	appendix
table of contents	glossary	index

Ask students which part of the book they would use to:

* find the copyright date
* find the author and illustrator
* look up the meaning of a word in the text
* find what page a map is on
* find special charts, references, etc.

Read the bulk of the information contained in the book.

© 1994 by Incentive Publications, Inc., Nashville, TN.

CRAZY TALK

Idioms are an interesting part of our language. Read these to your students and let them discuss the meaning of each:

in the nick of time	on pins and needles
passed with flying colors	have butterflies in your stomach
hit it off great	in one ear and out the other
didn't see eye to eye	on your high horse
spring a leak	chip off the old block
bury the hatchet	kick the bucket
bring home the bacon	lost his head
go through the roof	back to square one

© 1994 by Incentive Publications, Inc., Nashville, TN.

MONEY TALK

All the following sayings have to do with money. Let students discuss what they think each saying means. See if they can add other sayings to the list.

* He is a penny pincher. (He doesn't want to spend money or is very careful, thrifty.)

* It cost a pretty penny. (It was very expensive.)

* It cost an arm and a leg. (It was very expensive.)

* Money doesn't grow on trees. (Money has to be earned.)

© 1994 by Incentive Publications, Inc., Nashville, TN.

SAY WHEN

It isn't easy to get children to use some past tense verbs correctly. They often don't "sound" right because we are used to hearing them used incorrectly. Try a short drill occasionally with some of these often-misused verbs:

Present	Past	Past Participle
Today I . . .	*Yesterday I . . .*	*I have . . .*
see	saw	seen
take	took	taken
draw	drew	drawn
teach	taught	taught
do	did	done
go	went	gone
eat	ate	eaten

© 1994 by Incentive Publications, Inc., Nashville, TN.

-Q q R r S s · T t U u · V v · W w · X x · Y y Z z ·

I like to eat fruit.
Yesterday, I ate a pear.
I have eaten many pea

THINK FAST!

Impromptu speaking gives students a chance to think on their feet. Select one of the subjects below. Call on one student to talk on this subject for about one minute. Select a different subject for the next student. Add other subjects to the list for future talks.

Suggested subjects:

* ✱ You are a clock on the classroom wall. Describe your day.

* ✱ You are the principal of your school for today. What will you do?

* ✱ You are a pilgrim on the *Mayflower*. Tell about your trip.

* ✱ You will make all decisions about your family's meals for one week. Tell us about your decisions.

© 1994 by Incentive Publications, Inc., Nashville, TN.

GRAND SLAM!

Write one of these word family bases on the board. Ask for a student volunteer to "come to bat" with this word base.

Let the student score a single hit if he or she can add a blend to the base, a double hit if a suffix is then added, a triple hit if a prefix is also added, and a grand slam if the student can spell the final word. Then bring another student up to bat.

Word Family Bases:

ump	ail	ope	ake	ape	on
eep	ick	oat	ent	ack	id

© 1994 by Incentive Publications, Inc., Nashville, TN.

SYLLABLE RELAY

Separate the class into two teams. Ask for a one-syllable word from the first team. Then ask for a two-syllable word from the second team. Continue to alternate back and forth between the two teams, increasing the number of syllables each time.

Whenever a team cannot answer on its turn, the other team scores a point. Whichever team began second in the first round will begin first in the second round. Play until your time is gone or until one team scores five points.

Don't be surprised to find kids going through the dictionary in their spare time. They will want to be ready if they know they can play again soon.

© 1994 by Incentive Publications, Inc., Nashville, TN.

TOPIC TREASURES

Many times children find it difficult to begin writing a story or report because their topics are too broad.

Give students one of these broad topics and ask them to help you think of all possible related narrow topics.

Topics:

all about fish	TV shows	famous women	races
trains	inventions	music	careers
team sports	horses	automobiles	the space age

© 1994 by Incentive Publications, Inc., Nashville, TN.

LOOKING GOOD

Have students practice using good descriptive words with this activity. Select one distinctive character or person from the following list. Whisper that name to one student. That student must try to describe the character or person to the rest of the class without telling what the person or character does.

Superman

Santa Claus

Abraham Lincoln

George Washington

any popular cartoon character

any popular musician

Cupid

Statue of Liberty

any popular television character

© 1994 by Incentive Publications, Inc., Nashville, TN.

GOSSIP CHAIN

Use the old gossip game to show your students how things get changed as they are repeated over and over. Innocent people get hurt or may be embarrassed when facts are distorted.

Start one of these rumors to be whispered student to student around the room. Most will end up changed enough to make the point: spreading gossip is harmful.

* Susie's parents are getting a divorce because they don't love each other anymore (will probably end up that they don't love Susie anymore).

* Johnny got suspended from school because he was in a fight that started in Mr. White's room (will probably end up that Johnny started the fight).

© 1994 by Incentive Publications, Inc., Nashville, TN.

ALL ABOUT ME

Ask each student to write a brief description of him- or herself on paper. Have them pass the papers to you. Read aloud the description and see if the rest of the class can identify the student. Be sure to include a description of yourself.

This can be extended by assigning each paper a number. Post the descriptions on a bulletin board. Let each student number a paper to match the numbers on the descriptions. Then, through the day or over several days, students can list the students' names next to the number they think matches his or her description. Identify the correct names and let each student see how many he or she guessed correctly.

© 1994 by Incentive Publications, Inc., Nashville, TN.

POEMS IN A MINUTE

Formula poetry is easy to write and great for a class project. As you read aloud the requirement for a line, let the students decide what to write. Write it on the board as they compose it together.

Example:

Line 1: What are you writing about? *Butterflies.*

Line 2: Two adjectives to describe it. *Colorful and bright.*

Line 3: Two adverbs to tell how it acts. *Quietly, softly.*

Line 4: Two verbs to tell about it. *Flying and fluttering.*

Line 5: Tell how it makes you feel. *Makes me feel free.*

Line 6: Repeat what you're writing about. *Butterflies.*

© 1994 by Incentive Publications, Inc., Nashville, TN.

WEBBING WORDS

Write one word on the board. Decide whether you want students to think of synonyms, antonyms, or just words that are related to that word. As they name the type of words you've specified, add them to the board as a web around the original word.

Example: Healthy (name synonyms)

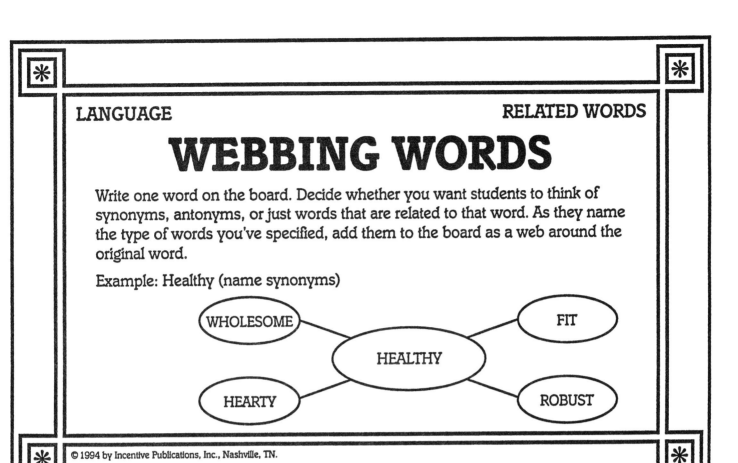

© 1994 by Incentive Publications, Inc., Nashville, TN.

MOODY WORDS

Let students take turns showing how they would look and act if one of these moody words described them:

frustrated	excited	embarrassed
cheerful	scared	defeated
angry	bewildered	proud
sad	ashamed	happy

© 1994 by Incentive Publications, Inc., Nashville, TN.

FILL IT FAST!

Quickly sketch a five-by-five square grid on the board. Make each section large enough to be able to write a word inside.

Ask students for a five-letter word to write above the squares of the grid horizontally. Then select a category to write next to each square vertically down the left side.

Challenge students to think of words to fit the categories that start with each of the letters of the horizontal word. Fill in the grid with the students' words as quickly as possible. Keep track of their record time and try to beat it the next time you play.

Categories: food, clothing, boys' or girls' names, states, rivers, animals, automobiles, TV shows, countries, or games

© 1994 by Incentive Publications, Inc., Nashville, TN.

SEEK AND FIND

To know everything is not possible, but to know where to find everything is important. This activity provides practice in selecting appropriate reference works for specific tasks.

Ask students to tell what reference work would be the best place to find the following information:

* population of your state
* name of the team that won the world series last year
* the author of *Charlotte's Web*
* meaning of the word "persimmon"
* the year that Thomas Edison was born
* who invented the typewriter
* the highest mountain in the United States
* how to pronounce "rendezvous"

© 1994 by Incentive Publications, Inc., Nashville, TN.

ALPHABET SOUP

1. Call on eight to ten students and ask each to give you a letter of the alphabet. Write the letters on the board as they are announced.

2. Give the class two minutes to make as many words as possible with the letters listed. Write them on the board as they call them out.

   Variation: Keep a set of index cards with one letter per card. Shuffle the deck and randomly select eight letters to write on the board. Proceed with Step 2 above.

© 1994 by Incentive Publications, Inc., Nashville, TN.

PROVE IT

Is it a fact or an opinion? Students often think that familiar opinions are actually fact. In this activity, students must decide whether each statement is an opinion or a fact. If they think it is a fact, they must be able to tell how to prove it. Try these:

* Canada and the United States share a border.

* Ice cream melts.

* Most students prefer chocolate milk to white milk.

* Roses smell good.

* _____ is a great singer. (Fill in name of any popular singer.)

* Solar energy can be used to cook hot dogs.

Add others to the list or let students add other statements.

© 1994 by Incentive Publications, Inc., Nashville, TN.

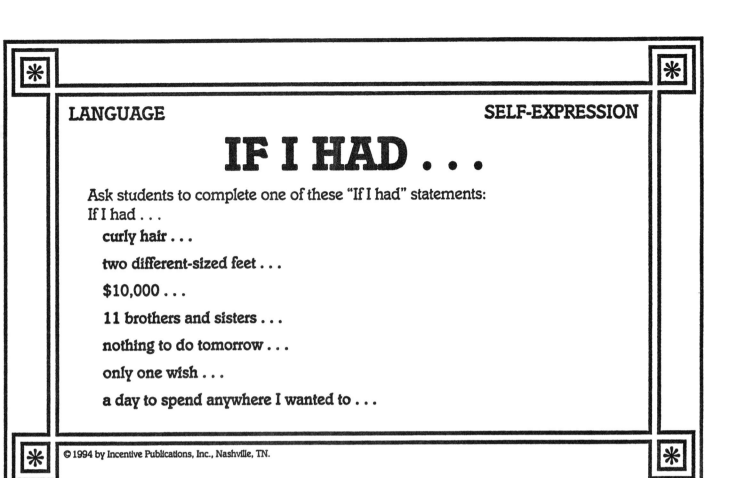

IF I HAD . . .

Ask students to complete one of these "If I had" statements:

If I had . . .

curly hair . . .

two different-sized feet . . .

$10,000 . . .

11 brothers and sisters . . .

nothing to do tomorrow . . .

only one wish . . .

a day to spend anywhere I wanted to . . .

© 1994 by Incentive Publications, Inc., Nashville, TN.

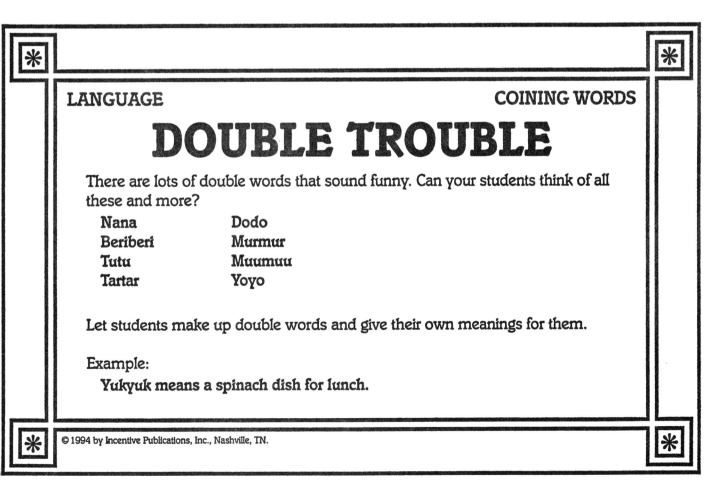

DOUBLE TROUBLE

There are lots of double words that sound funny. Can your students think of all these and more?

Nana	Dodo
Beriberi	Murmur
Tutu	Muumuu
Tartar	Yoyo

Let students make up double words and give their own meanings for them.

Example:

Yukyuk means a spinach dish for lunch.

© 1994 by Incentive Publications, Inc., Nashville, TN.

BOYS AND GIRLS

Lead a discussion of the advantages and disadvantages of being a boy or being a girl. Have girls tell what they consider the advantages of being a girl. Let them tell the disadvantages or problems with being female.

Then let boys discuss any advantages they think the girls have by being female. Be sure to give the girls equal time to state what they think is advantageous about being male.

© 1994 by Incentive Publications, Inc., Nashville, TN.

COUNTING FUN

Put some fun into oral counting practice. Count from one to the number of students in your class. Pair each number with a phrase using alliteration. Use a descriptive word and a noun with each number.

Example:

One Wonderful Waffle

Two Terrible Tempers

Three Thirsty Thumbs

Four Ferocious Footballs

© 1994 by Incentive Publications, Inc., Nashville, TN.

ALL IN THE FAMILY

List one of these word family bases on the board. Have students call out as many words as they can that use this word base. Remind them to use blends, prefixes, suffixes, and plural endings to make new words.

-at	**-ick**
-it	**-ack**
-all	**-act**
-ill	**-ad**
-ot	**-ate**

© 1994 by Incentive Publications, Inc., Nashville, TN.

CONTENTS SCAVENGER HUNT

Help students become familiar with their textbooks and practice using a table of contents. Have students take out a specific textbook and open it to the table of contents.

Ask questions like the ones listed here:

* ✳ What is the title of chapter three?
* ✳ On what page does chapter four begin?
* ✳ How many chapters are there in this book?
* ✳ What chapter has information about ___? (topic in that book)
* ✳ Is there an appendix?
* ✳ Is there a glossary? If so, on what page does it start?

© 1994 by Incentive Publications, Inc., Nashville, TN.

WORD PAIRS

Some words just always seem to be found together in our language. See how many of these word pairs your students are familiar with. Give the first part of the pair and let students supply the rest.

* ✳ cup and <u>saucer</u>
* ✳ bright-eyed and <u>bushy-tailed</u>
* ✳ sugar and <u>spice</u>
* ✳ strange but <u>true</u>
* ✳ spic and <u>span</u>
* ✳ huff and <u>puff</u>
* ✳ hide and <u>seek</u>
* ✳ peace and <u>quiet</u>
* ✳ sticks and <u>stones</u>
* ✳ aches and <u>pains</u>

If these are too easy, try a few word triplets:

* ✳ bacon, <u>lettuce</u>, and <u>tomato</u>
* ✳ hop, <u>skip</u>, and <u>jump</u>
* ✳ animal, <u>vegetable</u>, or <u>mineral</u>
* ✳ tall, <u>dark</u>, and <u>handsome</u>

© 1994 by Incentive Publications, Inc., Nashville, TN.

YELLOW IS FOR JELLO?

To practice categorizing objects, select a color or shape and ask students to name as many things as they can that would normally be that color or shape. Keep going until no one can think of another object in that category. Some students will really stretch their imaginations (and yours).

Possible Categories:

* things that are green . . . grass, money, spinach, mold

* things that are round . . . sun, oranges, clock, zero

* things that are red . . . strawberries, blood, roses, tired eyes

* things that are rectangular . . . tissue box, textbook, door, window

© 1994 by Incentive Publications, Inc., Nashville, TN.

IN THE MIDDLE

Write one of these pairs of guide words on the board. Ask students to name all the words they can think of that would fit on a dictionary page with those guide words. If anyone challenges a word offered, write that word on the board between the guide words so the class can decide if it belongs there.

Guide word pairs:

sand ....slide	help...........house	laugh..........lint
baby..........bed	you............zip	stutter........swift
pin ....plant	bullet.........cent	act ....art
tea.............train	man...........middle	fast ....fence

© 1994 by Incentive Publications, Inc., Nashville, TN.

HEAD OF THE LINE

Have your students line up somewhere in the room. Start with the last student in the line. Ask for an example from one of the language categories given below. If the student is able to give an example that is correct, that student moves to the head of the line. Change categories frequently within the five-minute period.

a contraction	a noun
a prefix	an abbreviation
a suffix	a word beginning with QU
a preposition	a compound word
an adverb	a pair of homonyms
a word with Z	a word and its antonym

© 1994 by Incentive Publications, Inc., Nashville, TN.

UNCOMMONLY GOOD

Select a common item that is well-known by almost all the students. Discuss its common uses. Then encourage students to use their imaginations in thinking of uncommon ways to use the item.

Example: **toothbrush (for brushing teeth)**

Uncommon uses: to brush a hamster, to scrub potatoes, to clean jewelry, as a hockey stick for a hamster

Other common commonalities to try:

safety pin	toothpick	pencil	paper clip
fork	spoon	tissue	tack
nail file	comb	broom	straw

© 1994 by Incentive Publications, Inc., Nashville, TN.

WONDER-FULL

Encourage your students to vocalize their "I wonder . . ." thoughts. Let each student tell one thing about which he or she wonders. The thoughts may be serious or they may be on the silly side.

If you have time, write these thoughts on a large sheet of tagboard or craft paper for the bulletin board. Students can continue to add to the list. They can also write great creative stories based on the wonder list.

I wonder . . .

- . . . how many stars there are
- . . . why the colors in the rainbow are always the same
- . . . why my parents picked this name for me
- . . . which really came first: the chicken or the egg
- . . . what my teacher does after school

© 1994 by Incentive Publications, Inc., Nashville, TN.

SEASONAL SEARCH

When it is time to line up, let each student earn a place in line by giving you a vocabulary word that is appropriate for the current season or holiday.
Example:

Fall: leaves, autumn, pumpkin, witch, Halloween
Winter: Christmas, snow, cold, icicles, sled

Lists could also be made for a particular subject or concept that you are currently studying.

To extend the activity, as each student gives a word, ask for a volunteer to spell it.

© 1994 by Incentive Publications, Inc., Nashville, TN.

MOUSE, MICE . . . HOUSE, HICE?

Irregular words are hard for students to remember. Use this list to review irregular plurals. Call out the singular form of the word and ask students to name the plural form.

mouse . . . mice

goose . . . geese

fish . . . fish or fishes

deer . . . deer

die . . . dice (most children use dice as singular and plural)

child . . . children

woman . . . women

© 1994 by Incentive Publications, Inc., Nashville, TN.

DESCRIPTION DILEMMA

Have students name an interesting animal or object, or select one from the list below. Write the name of the object on the board vertically. Students should think of verbs to describe how it might move (if it's an animal) or adjectives to describe the object itself. Think of one for each letter in the name of the object.

Example: Hamster

Harmless	Mild-Mannered	Terrific	Restless
Active	Silly	Energetic	

Other word choices:

dinosaur	unicorn	computer
leprechaun	dragon	ostrich
bullfrog	platypus	ghost

© 1994 by Incentive Publications, Inc., Nashville, TN.

The ball soared past second base because....

WHAT HAPPENED?

Have students examine cause and effect relationships by completing these statements to tell what happened next.

I was hungry so . . .   Jack put hot fudge sauce on
Strong winds blew and . . .   the ice cream and it . . .
I felt sick so I . . .

Now change the activity around. Have students finish the same statements so that the part they add is the cause rather than the effect:

I was hungry because . . .   Jack put hot fudge sauce on
Strong winds blew when . . .   the ice cream because . . .
I felt sick after . . .

© 1994 by Incentive Publications, Inc., Nashville, TN.

SELF-AWARENESS
SELF-AWARENESS
SELF-AWARENESS
SELF-AWARENESS

SELF-AWARENESS   GET-ACQUAINTED ACTIVITY

ONE MINUTE TO GO

This is a great "get to know me" activity to do during the first few weeks of school.

Bring one student to the front of the room. Let that student talk about him- or herself for one minute. Ask the student to include information about family, hobbies, likes and dislikes, etc.

Repeat with three or four other students each day. Let the whole class become acquainted with each other in just two weeks. Don't forget to include yourself!

© 1994 by Incentive Publications, Inc., Nashville, TN.

FLY ME!

Let each student write a self-description or a list of favorite things on a piece of paper with no name on it.

Then let each student form a paper airplane from the paper and instruct them to fly their airplanes across the room.

Each student may pick up one airplane, read the list aloud, and try to identify the writer.

© 1994 by Incentive Publications, Inc., Nashville, TN.

WHICH SIDE?

Give your restless students an opportunity to move around and make some choices at the same time.

Have all the students move to one side of the room. Then tell them that they must choose only one of the two things you announce. All students choosing the same thing move to one side of the room. All others move to the other side of the room. Then announce two more things to choose from and let them move accordingly.

candy bar or ice cream	horse or motorbike
pencil or paper	hamster or parakeet
movie or video game	chess set or checker game
swimming pool or boat	hamburger or pizza

© 1994 by Incentive Publications, Inc., Nashville, TN.

HIDDEN FRIENDS

Ask students: "How does it make you feel when someone does something nice for you? What kinds of things can you do for someone else that don't cost money or take much time? What things do you like other people to do for you?"

Let students write their names on slips of paper and pass them to you. Then let everyone draw out one slip, making sure that no one gets his or her own name.

Explain that in the next day or so you would like each person to try to do some simple "nice thing" for the person whose name was drawn. The deed should be done without mention of the fact that the student drew that name. Two days later discuss what was done and the feelings that resulted.

© 1994 by Incentive Publications, Inc., Nashville, TN.

I CAN! I CAN!

Are you tired of hearing your students say "I can't"? Provide each of them an opportunity to say, "I can!"

Go around the room quickly, letting one student at a time tell something he or she can do. It doesn't have to be something earth-shaking—just making a positive statement about their abilities will be earth-shaking enough for some students. Being positive can be as habit-forming as being negative. Try to repeat this activity at least once every two or three weeks during the school year.

© 1994 by Incentive Publications, Inc., Nashville, TN.

ONLY ME

Encourage each student in your class to explore his or her own uniqueness. Have students stand, one at a time, and tell one thing about him- or herself that is unique.

Set the tone for an accepting atmosphere in which each student can feel comfortable sharing personal information.

Examples of "uniqueness":

    I have seven sisters and brothers.
    My eyes are two different colors.
    I broke my leg last week.

© 1994 by Incentive Publications, Inc., Nashville, TN.

COMPLIMENT CHAIN

Form a human compliment chain. It helps young people learn to give compliments and to accept compliments graciously.

Have the first student turn to the next student and pay him or her a sincere compliment. The complimented student should say "thank you" and then turn to the next student and compliment him or her. Continue the chain until the last student has complimented the first student.

An independent project that is a good follow-up to this is to have students write several compliments for one person on paper strips and form a paper compliment chain from the strips. The chain could be given to the person about whom the compliments were written.

© 1994 by Incentive Publications, Inc., Nashville, TN.

SELF-AWARENESS   COMMON ATTRIBUTES

JUST LIKE ME

Select two students to stand in front of the room. Each student then selects another student to stand by his or her side and tells one way in which that student is just like him- or herself. Continue taking turns until no students remain to be called or until one of the students cannot find another student that is like him or her in some way. Be sure to discuss the likenesses as attributes that they share.

Another version would be to have only one student come to the front of the room. That student selects a classmate that is "just like me" in some way. Then the second student calls on a student to compare to and so on.

 © 1994 by Incentive Publications, Inc., Nashville, TN.

SELF-AWARENESS   OBSERVATION

SHOE BUSINESS

How observant are your students? Do they really notice each other? Find out with this activity (best for a time when students are restless and need a little fun). Have everyone stand where they can see each other for one minute. Then have everyone take off their shoes and place them in front of the class (be sure to keep pairs together).

Hold up one pair at a time and see if someone other than the owner can match them with the correct student.

Promise to repeat the activity sometime next week. Watch students keep an eye on each other.

 © 1994 by Incentive Publications, Inc., Nashville, TN.